SPARTANBURG
REVISITED

SPARTANBURG REVISITED

A Second Look at
the Photographs of
Alfred & Bob Willis

HUB CITY
writers project
2007

Contemporary Images by
Carroll Foster & Mark Olencki

Introduction by Emily L. Smith

First printing, November 2007

Front cover—Alfred Willis's late 1920s image of a deserted Magnolia Street at dusk shows the old County Courthouse and the Hotel Morgan, then known as the Gresham Hotel, in the distance.
Title page—Negative image: The Cleveland Law Range, built in the late 1880s on Magnolia Street, served as home to the various business interests of John B. and Jesse Cleveland. It had been standing for more 50 years when Alfred Willis took this photograph.
    2007 image: The Law Range is still owned by a descendant of the Cleveland brothers, and a few offices remain there. A live oak grows in front of the building today. —Mark Olencki
Back cover—2007 view down Magnolia Street —Mark Olencki
Cover & book design—Mark Olencki
Project editor—Betsy Teter
Copy editor—Carol Bradof
Printed in China

Library of Congress Cataloging-in-Publication Data

Willis, Alfred, 1880-1945.
Spartanburg revisited : a second look at the photographs of Alfred and Bob Willis / introduction by Emily L. Smith ; contemporary photography by Carroll Foster and Mark Olencki.
        p. cm.
ISBN-13: 978-1-891885-56-3 (pbk. : alk. paper)
ISBN-13: 978-1-891885-57-0 (hardback : alk. paper)
1. Spartanburg (S.C.)—History—Pictorial works. 2. Spartanburg (S.C.)—Pictorial works. 3. Spartanburg (S.C.)—Biography—Pictorial works. 4. Willis, Alfred, 1880-1945—Family—Pictorial works. 5. Historic sites—South Carolina—Spartanburg—Pictorial works. 6. Historic buildings—South Carolina—Spartanburg—Pictorial works. 7. Spartanburg (S.C.)—Buildings, structures, etc.—Pictorial works. 8. Willis, Alfred, 1880-1945. 9. Willis, Bob, d. 1993. 10. Photographers—South Carolina—Spartanburg—Biography. I. Willis, Bob, d. 1993. II. Foster, Carroll, 1972- III. Olencki, Mark, 1953- IV. Title.

F279.S7W55 2007
975.7'290440222—dc22

2007020386

Hub City Writers Project
Post Office Box 8421
Spartanburg, South Carolina 29305
(864) 577-9349 • fax (864) 577-0188 • www.hubcity.org

Spartanburg Revisited is underwritten in part
by the Spartanburg County Public Libraries,
which houses the Willis Photography Collection.

DONORS

THE REVEREND AND MRS. DAVID FORT
MR. ROGER MILLIKEN
THE PHIFER/JOHNSON FOUNDATION
THE SPARTANBURG COUNTY PUBLIC LIBRARIES
THE SOUTH CAROLINA ARTS COMMISSION

The Arts Partnership of Greater Spartanburg
Paula and Stan Baker
Dwight and Liz Patterson

Monta and Ken Anthony
Valerie and Bill Barnet
Carol and Jim Bradof
Bea and Dennis L. Bruce
Mr. and Mrs. M. L. Cates Jr.
Sally and Jerry Cogan Jr.
Justin and Anna Converse

Paul and Nancy Coté
Nancy Crowley
Andy and Lynne Falatok
Dr. and Mrs. John Featherston
Donald L. Fowler
Bill James

Byron McCane
Tom and Nan McDaniel
Norman Powers
Rose Mary Ritchie
John Lane and Betsy Teter
Bette Wakefield
Dennis and Annemarie Wiseman

Margaret Allen
Dr. and Mrs. Mitch Allen
Mr. and Mrs. Robert Allen
Mack and Patty Amick
Callis and Pamela Anderson, Jr.
Tom and Ceci Arthur
Mr. and Mrs. Robert Atkins
Greg and Lisa Atkins
Becky Bagwell
Mr. and Mrs. W. D. Bain, Jr.
Susan Baker
First South Bank
Tom and Joan Barnet
Charles and Christi Bebko

Kathie and Roy Bennett
Victor and Linda Bilanchone
Clarke and Martha Blackman
Shirley Blaes
Bob and Jennifer Bourguignon
Walter Brice
Mellnee G. Buchheit
William and Katherine Burns
Katherine and Marvin Cann
Terry and Janis Cash
Ruth L. Cate
Martha Chapman
Harrison Chapman
Nan and Tim Cleveland

Mr. and Mrs. Richard Conn
Mike and Nancy Corbin
Helen and Ben Correll
Tom Moore Craig
Ronald and Liz Crawley
John and Kirsten Cribb
Daniel and Becky Cromer
Betsy Cox and Mike Curtis
Fran and Tom Davis
Wilhelmina S. Dearybury
David Dedmon
Fredrick B. Dent
Mr. and Mrs. Magruder H. Dent
Georgie and Bill Dickerson

Chris and Alice Dorrance
David Drum
Dave and Sandy Edwards
Stewart and Anne Elliott
Dr. and Mrs. William C. Elston
Ginger and Bob Elwell
Edwin Epps
The Rev. Beth and Mr. Duncan Ely
Max and Ann Fain
Dr. and Mrs. George Fields Jr.
Elsie Finkelstein
Vivian Fisher
Dr. and Mrs. Harold Fleming
Russel and Susan Floyd
Kimberly Anne and Ashley Fly
Will and Liz Fort
Caleb and Delie Fort
Alton Foster
Lorelei Foster
The Frame Up
Elaine Freeman
Mr. and Mrs. William P. Gee
Marsha and Jimmy Gibbs
Margaret and Chip Green
Mr. and Mrs. Tom Grier
Lucy Grier
Jim and Kay Gross
Marianna and Roger Habisreutinger
Lee and Kitty Hagglund
Ibrahim Hanif
Tom and Tracy Hannah
Peyton and Michele Harvey
Eaddy Williams Hayes
Gary and Carmela Henderson
Mike and Nancy Henderson
Susan Hodge
Mr. and Mrs. Tom Hollis
Marion Peter Holt
Doug and Marilyn Hubbell
Erin Hubbell
Mr. and Mrs. Kenneth R. Huckaby
Woodrow and Carol Hughes
Debra Hutchins
David and Harriet Ike
Susan B. Jackson
Sadie Jackson
Dr. and Mrs. Vernon Jeffords

William Jeffords
Tom Johnson
Wallace Eppes Johnson
Mr. and Mrs. Charles W. Jones
Mr. and Mrs. Daniel Kahrs
Mr. and Mrs. Jay H. Kaplan
Mr. and Mrs. Kim Keith
Dr. Ann J. Kelly
Dr. and Mrs. Bert Knight
Mary Jane and Cecil Lanford
Mr. and Mrs. Jack W. Lawrence
Dr. and Mrs. Wood and Janice Lay
Joe and Ruth Lesesne
Francie and Lindsay Little
Bruce Littlejohn
George and Frances Loudon
Brownlee and Julie Lowry
Manning and Mary Speed Lynch
Robert and Nancy Lyon
Dr. and Mrs. Nathaniel Magruder
Zerno E. Martin Jr.
Bill and Wendy Mayrose
Fayssoux Dunbar McLean
Gail D. McCullough
Dr. and Mrs. Larry T. McGehee
Thomas and Chapman McMeekin
Bob McMichael
Ed and Gail Medlin
Boyce and Carole Miller
Mr. and Mrs. Charles Minch
Karen and Bob Mitchell
Teddy and Lynne Monroe
George D. Mullinax
Carrie Duello and Joe Mullinax
Mr. and Mrs. Douglas B. Nash
Cecile and Chris Nowatka
Corry and Amy Oakes
Steve O'Neill
Geneva F. Padgett
Frazer S. M. Pajak
Mr. and Mrs. W. Keith Parris
Richard Pennell
Mr. and Mrs. Edward P. Perrin
John and Lynne Poole
Jan and Sara Lynn Postma Jr.
Mr. and Mrs. L. Perrin Powell
Barbara Powell

Harold P. Powell
Elizabeth and W.O. Pressley Jr.
Harry Price
Norman and Jo Pulliam
Eileen Rampey
Allison and John Ratterree
Melissa Walker and Chuck Reback
Harriette and Marty Reid
Alex and Farrah Richardson
Elisabeth and Regis Robe
Martial and Amy Robichaud
Ronald and Peggy Romine
Steve and Elena Rush
S&ME Inc.
B. Holland Satterfield Jr.
John and Sue Scott
Garrett and Cathy Scott
Tony and Flonnie Shaw
Mr. and Mrs. Clyde O. Smith
James Ross Snell Jr.
Betty B. Snow
Debra Spear
Sarah J. Spencer
Sara Hamilton and Brad Steinecke
Dr. and Mrs. B.G. Stephens
Mr. and Mrs. David L. Steven
Tammy and David Stokes
Phillip Stone
Mr. and Mrs. George Stone
Chris and Jessalyn Story
Christine and Bob Swager
Nancy Taylor
Ray Thompson
Mr. and Mrs. Mike Trammell
Mr. and Mrs. J.W. Wakefield, Jr.
Bill and Winnie Walsh
David and Kathy Weir
Dave and Linda Whisnant
Mary K. Wilborn
Alanna and Don Wildman
Jeffrey R. Willis
Mary G. Willis
Mr. and Mrs. James Wilson
Bob and Carolyn Wynn
Elizabeth York
Elizabeth H. Young
Suzanne and Jon Zoole

Alfred Willis, one of the first commercial photographers in upstate South Carolina, kept a studio on East Main Street near Morgan Square from the mid-1920s to the early 1930s. This photograph is taken along that stretch of the street during those years.

INTRODUCTION
by Emily L. Smith

In the spring of 2006, Spartanburg photographers Carroll Foster and Mark Olencki met with Hub City Writers Project founders John Lane and Betsy Teter on the balcony of Wild Wing Café. The two commercial photographers had long admired the early-mid twentieth century images of Spartanburg father and son photographers Alfred Tennyson Willis and Robert Henry "Bob" Willis. After a serendipitous meeting in 2003 with Alfred Willis's daughter Elizabeth "Lib" Willis Fowler, Carroll Foster had devoted several years to helping restore two trunks full of her father's negatives. A Willis enthusiast and collector, Mark Olencki had shared office space in the 1980s with Bob Willis, who was then in his mid seventies. The veteran photographer instantly became his mentor. Between their combined work with archival Willis photographs and their respective collections of memorabilia, Mark and Carroll had compiled a loose Willis family history and believed the material merited a book. In honor and celebration of Alfred and Bob's enduring contributions to Spartanburg, the two photographers proposed "re-shooting" some of the scenes depicted in the Willises' images, a look at Spartanburg "then and now." For the first time, vintage Willis photographs would appear alongside contemporary versions of existing street corners and buildings.

The compilation of photographs known as the Willis Collection traces over eighty years of Spartanburg's bustling downtown, mills, military camps, and churches, as well as the people and activities that breathed life into them. "I have almost a brick by brick account of it," Alfred Willis remarked in 1936 of the weekly progress pictures he made during the construction of Spartanburg High School. The same might be said of his beloved Spartanburg. Among his

Bob Willis and traveling companion, Zack, in the Dean Street studio

most celebrated images is the rare one of treasured Spartanburg street entertainer George Mullins, better known locally as Trottin' Sally, as well as ones of the historic visits of aviator Charles Lindbergh and evangelist Billy Sunday.

Born in Williston, South Carolina in 1880 to Robert Henry and Jessie T. Willis, Alfred was one of the first commercial photographers in upstate South Carolina. When he died in 1945, he passed the camera to his then thirty-year-old son Bob, already a budding portrait photographer. Like his father before him, Bob continued to preserve Spartanburg in images until his own death in 1993. In many cases, their photographs are the only remaining record of Spartanburg's past: its landmarks, its people, and its momentous occasions.

As the photographers and publishers sat, fittingly, looking out across a recently reconfigured and restored Morgan Square, Willis photographs of Spartanburg sprang to mind—downtown's Morgan Square in various incarnations, the Franklin Hotel, Duncan Park Stadium, Hammond-Brown-Jennings Furniture store complete with 1930s-era cars parked out back, First Baptist Church, and a 1920s train departing the station, among many. Some structures stood exactly as they had for decades; others had been erased entirely. Carroll Foster conceived of the project as "the enlightenment of what we've done with our city—good and bad."

When deciding which photographs to include, Carroll and Mark considered whether they could create an artful and compelling new version. They considered whether re-photographing the Willises' originals would make a statement or inspire viewers to think about Spartanburg's future. Through the resulting photographs, they ask us to reflect on what we've left behind, as well as on what remains. "With what could we replace it?" Carroll poses, "if there's nothing left but a dirt patch or a run down gas station?"

* * *

The two photographers had just embarked on the massive project of re-shooting some 50 Willis images when I came on board. A native South

Alfred Willis was present when city officials broke ground on a snowy day in 1930 for a new post office on Magnolia Street. The building, which still stands, is now known as the Federal Building.

Carolinian, I moved to Spartanburg in June to serve as the Hub City Writers Project's first writer-in-residence. By late summer I had signed on to write the introduction to what was then dubbed simply "the Willis book" and began eagerly tagging along with the photographers on assignments.

On a warm, early September afternoon, I accompanied Carroll Foster on one of his first outings. We stopped first at the Coca-Cola bottling plant on West Main Street to inquire about borrowing a van to recreate Alfred Willis's photograph of a Chero-Cola truck parked in Morgan Square. Bottled in Spartanburg and a Coca-Cola competitor (though Coca-Cola was first with a local plant), Chero-Cola dates to a time when numerous companies bottled colas. The receptionist asked us to jot down our contact information and indicated that a Coca-Cola representative would be in touch. Next we stood in line at the post office on Church Street, gave our spiel, and were ushered into the postmaster's office, where we were delighted to discover Alfred Willis's 1920s-era photograph of postal carriers hanging on the wall. The postmaster immediately agreed to a re-shoot. A week later, Carroll returned around eight a.m., before the bustle of mail routes, to photograph his 2006 version. Just before I met him, Carroll had photographed what could have been the final season of Duncan Park baseball. Host to professional minor league teams from its inception in 1926 until 1994, and occasionally even to baseball greats such as Joe DiMaggio and Lou Gehrig, the park hosted the Spartanburg Stingers, a collegiate wooden bat summer league, the evening Carroll was there. Following the summer 2006 season, city officials announced the stadium would be padlocked.

* * *

If I could do it, I'd do no writing at all," James Agee professed in his textual portrait of 1930s sharecroppers, *Let Us Now Praise Famous Men*. "It would be photographs." As Mark, Carroll, Betsy, and I began to juxtapose the Willis originals and the "revisited" images, the story of Spartanburg, indeed, took shape—its history in images. The photographs, "then and now," spoke

Spartanburg attorney Ibra Blackwood on the stump in one of his two gubernatorial campaigns. He was elected on his second try in 1931 and served four years, and Alfred Willis captured him on film.

From the 1920s until the 1950s H. R. "Red" Dobson coached most sports at Spartanburg High School. Here he poses for Alfred Willis with a 1920s-era tumbling team.

for themselves. But there was a spark that leapt from one artist to another, one medium to another, a yearning to give voice to our mutual curiosity and experiences. As Mark and Carroll continued shooting, I combed through old yearbooks, obituaries, and articles, and met with Alfred and Bob Willis's family members and friends. It became clear to all of us: the Willises' legacy was greater than any compilation of their photographs.

There was the story of the original Willis Collection, sold to the Spartanburg *Herald-Journal* in the early 1980s. Then, the 2005 addition of some six hundred lost photographs and negatives, many of which were nearly discarded. There was the unexpected discovery of amateur photographs taken by Alfred Willis's elder brother, Lieutenant Colonel Robert Henry Willis, Junior—proof of a third Willis photographer. There was also the longstanding relationship between contemporary photographers Carroll Foster and Mark Olencki and the Willis photographers and their photographs.

And then there were the Willises themselves. Around Spartanburg the mere mention of their names incited anecdotes about the father/son school picture takers and of the laughter and magic they created around them everywhere they went. People remembered their cars, their dogs, their yards, their jokes, and their trademark idiosyncrasies. Along with Mark and Carroll, I, too, fell in love with the Willises—the charismatic and affable men I met through their images and the surviving Willis family members who so generously shared them with me.

While *Spartanburg Revisited* is undeniably a tribute to the city that fills these pages, it is also homage to the two men who recorded her past. In photograph after photograph, their stories brimmed; Alfred and Bob Willis deserved an accompanying text.

THE WILLIS COLLECTION

The Willis Collection garnered widespread recognition in Spartanburg through a late 1980s *Herald-Journal* column called "Yesteryear." The photographs, which were purchased by the newspaper in 1984 from Alfred Willis's son Bob, and later donated in their entirety to the Spartanburg County Libraries, have since been widely used to accompany history texts and illustrate an ever-changing Spartanburg. Hub City Writers Project author Philip N. Racine drew heavily from the Collection when compiling his 1999 book *Seeing Spartanburg: A History in Images*. Sixty-two years after Alfred Willis's death, his images have found their way onto the world wide web and now grace the City of Spartanburg's website. Eight-foot enlargements of Trottin' Sally, the Spartanburg High tumbling team in pyramid formation, and pedestrians informally gathered in Morgan Square to exchange the day's business and weather reports, welcome visitors to the main branch of the library.

But even as the donation of original Willis prints and glass-plate negatives to the Spartanburg County Libraries secured their critical climate controlled storage, ensured renewed viewership, and introduced the names Alfred and Bob Willis to a new generation of Spartanburg residents, an undiscovered cache of some 600 glass negatives and prints remained buried inside of two family trunks. Following the 1982 death of Alfred Willis's second wife, Lucille Miller, his youngest daughter, Elizabeth "Lib" Willis Fowler, inherited the trunks and moved them into her Boiling Springs home. She knew they contained negatives and even presented a box to her half-brother Bob, who warned her of the hazardous nature of negatives printed on nitrate. He suggested she discard them. "Well, I discarded them," Lib remembers, "and then I thought, you know, the trunk is there; the trunk is taking up space. They fit in the trunk, and so I put them back." That's where they remained until 2003 when Lib stopped by the Spartanburg photography studio of Steve Fincher to have her portrait made. While waiting for Steve, Lib noticed a young photographer restoring a glass-plate negative and mentioned to him the trunks full of Willis family ephemera. Carroll Foster, who didn't realize when he met Lib that she was the daughter of Alfred Willis, had long looked up to Willis as one of the founding fathers of photography in the area. "But I assumed since Alfred Willis died over sixty years ago, and his son Bob had died, I would never know anybody in the family." A week later a nervous Carroll called Lib to ask if he could see the

Over 600 lost Willis photographs and glass negatives, articles, receipts, and high school yearbooks were discovered in two trunks in the Boiling Springs home of Alfred Willis's youngest daughter Elizabeth "Lib" Willis Fowler. Known as "Uncle Henry's trunk" to Willis family members, the oldest of the pair belonged to Alfred Willis's brother Lieutenant Colonel Robert Henry Willis, Jr.

collection. "When Carroll called me, I thought he was calling to harass me because I hadn't made a decision on which picture I wanted," Lib chuckles. The rest, as they say, is history.

Together Lib, Steve Fincher, and Carroll Foster unpacked the trunks full of lost Willis photographs, negatives, articles, receipts, pamphlets, advertisements, maps, and high school yearbooks, some of which even Lib had never before seen. "I'd grab things and bring boxes in from the bedroom," Lib recalls. "Carroll and Steve and I would sit in the floor and go through it." While most of the Willis family mementos were returned to the trunk's miniature drawers for safekeeping, Steve and Carroll spent two years meticulously cleaning and restoring several hundred delicate glass plates, silver nitrate negatives, and prints to turn over to the Spartanburg County Public Libraries. The resulting photographs, many of which appear in this book's "Willis Family Album," have, until now, never been published. More so than the celebrated street-scapes and architectural shots, these candid portraits of friends, family and, especially of Alfred Willis's eight children, bring his personality and sense of humor to light.

* * *

Like many Spartanburg locals, Susan Brown can remember saying "whistle britches" for her Granddaddy Robert H. "Bob" Willis just before he took her class picture as a girl at Pine Street School. For those who attended school in Spartanburg County, the Willis name is synonymous with picture day. Older generations, too, tell stories of the charismatic Mr. Willis taking their annual portraits, superlatives and team sports photos. Do the math, though, and this "Mr. Willis" would have to have been more than a hundred years old. "Like many people, I was confused initially," even Carroll Foster admits. "Many times photographs were identified simply as Willis Collection or Willis/*Herald-Journal* Collection." Alfred and Bob's photographs, much like the photographers, bleed together, Carroll believes, because their prints and negatives were packaged as a set.

By 1934 Alfred Willis had moved to 153$^{1/2}$ North Church, the studio for which he is probably best known. The brick building, which was torn down in the early '80s, stood between the Hammond-Brown-Jennings furniture store on the corner of St. John and North Church Streets and the present site of Control Data's Business Technology Center at 145 North Church.

When Alfred Willis died, his son, Bob Willis, inherited Willis Studio, then at 153$^{1/2}$ North Church Street. Under Bob's ownership, the business grew and moved several times, eventually to Dean Street where it was located until Bob died in 1993 and Willis Studio closed its doors for good. Like his father before him, Bob Willis began as a portrait photographer. Alfred sent his son to study at the well-established Manning Studios in Greenville, with which he had been associated early in his own photographic career. Bob assumed his father's role as official Spartanburg County schools' photographer when Alfred died. He continued to take class pictures until at least the mid-sixties, after which he began to focus exclusively on industrial photography for Duke Power. The original Willis Collection, as compiled by Bob Willis and sold to the *Herald-Journal*, always featured the photographs of both father and son.

The opening of the trunks, though, confirmed yet another Willis photographer. The oldest of the trunks, known to Lib as "Uncle Henry's trunk," contained the brittle and yellowing personal documents of Alfred's brother, Lieutenant Colonel Robert Henry Willis, Jr. The first honor graduate in The Citadel's class of 1908 and a pilot in World War I, Henry was killed in France in 1918, just six days after his thirty-second birthday. An amateur photographer, he documented his travels through San Diego, Texas, Mexico, France, and other places where he was stationed. Steve and Carroll were able to identify, among other attractions, the historic beachfront Hotel Del Coronado in San Diego, the federal penitentiary Alcatraz, and Fort Sam Houston, where Henry was hospitalized following a plane crash. Although his photographs mostly portray glimpses of life beyond Spartanburg, it is thanks to Henry that candid images of his rarely photographed brother Alfred exist.

BEHIND THE CURTAIN: ALFRED AND BOB WILLIS

*I*t's adventurous," Alfred Willis said in an interview for Spartanburg High's *Scribbler* newspaper regarding his life as a photographer. "You get to see and do things, and it's never monotonous," he remarked. "I'm made with a craving

Crowds of people lined both sides of Magnolia Street in this Alfred Willis image from the 1920s. The statue of Daniel Morgan was flanked by cannons and cannon balls in those days. The county courthouse, the Hotel Morgan, and the Cleveland Law Range are featured in the distant skyline.

After finding the perfect location for the above Spartanburg High School annual "feature," which called for a girl sitting in the woods near a waterfall, Alfred Willis planted ferns and cut dogwood for decoration. When he printed his photograph, though, he couldn't see the waterfall. He searched until he found a photograph he had taken several years earlier of a waterfall, but this time, the water in the image flowed in the wrong direction. Look closely, and you might notice where Alfred resourcefully flipped the prints over backwards on the other picture and photographed the result.

for adventure." Leaning forward in his chair, he continued, "Lots of times I'm waked up at night to get pictures of the scene of a crime for use in court. There's plenty of variety and excitement in this business." When asked about memories of her father, Lib Willis Fowler immediately remembers driving with him to her mother's family home in Walnut Grove when he spotted a cloud that looked like a woman with her hair blowing in the breeze. Alfred pulled over, stopped the car, and set up his camera to photograph it. Mind you, Fowler recalls, this was in the early 1940s, and Alfred couldn't simply lean out of his window and snap a picture. Cameras at the time were cumbersome to adjust and to shoot.

By the early 1930s Alfred Willis was not only responsible for Spartanburg High School's annual portraits but also for staging elaborate features, which he called "desserts," with themes such as "Coming Through Rye," "Travels with a Donkey," and "Milton." The last called for photographing a girl sitting in the woods near a waterfall, dreaming over a book. After finding the perfect wooded location sloping down to the water, Alfred planted ferns and cut dogwood for decoration. When he printed the photograph, though, he couldn't see the water. He searched until he found a photograph he had taken several years earlier of a waterfall, but this time, the water in the image flowed in the wrong direction. "So what did I do," he said, "but flop the prints over backwards on the other picture, photograph the result, and there was my picture."

The photographer with an insatiable craving for adventure also collected guns and was a tremendous marksman. Daughters Lucy, Rachael, Edith, and Lib often accompanied him when he went skeet shooting. He had a passion for unusual artifacts and owned, among other things, spears, an ostrich egg, and a miniature signal cannon out of which he shot blanks on New Year's Eve. It now sits at the foot of his daughter Lib's fireplace, where her granddaughter loads it with marbles. Lib says Alfred once owned the first gun made in South Carolina; it was subsequently stolen out of his car. He bequeathed her a pearl-handled pistol, a reminder of the song "Pistol Packin' Momma," which they mutually loved. The youngest of his eight children, she was only six years old then, but the memory and the song's lyrics are vivid. "Oh, drinkin' beer in a cabaret, was I havin' fun. Until one night she caught me right, and now I'm on the run," she sings. Alfred often took her to the diner near his studio at 153$^{1/2}$ North Church Street and placed a shiny nickel in her palm to play it on the jukebox. "I don't know what kind of song this was for a little girl to listen to," she laughs now.

After a four-year naval career that included stints in Europe, Arabia, Ethiopia, and also in the Spanish American War, twenty-five-year-old Alfred Willis returned to his native South Carolina and purchased an interest in a Union drug store. He remained there until 1909, when he moved to Charleston to work at Laurens Art Store. Photographs of such Charleston attractions as the Battery attest to Alfred's then growing interest in photography. He moved to Spartanburg in 1912 and opened a Kodak finishing plant at Ligon's Drug Store, where he worked until 1919. He was associated with Manning portrait studios of Greenville for three years and, in 1922, went into business for himself, specializing in commercial photography. In 1926, he operated a studio at 115$^{1/2}$ East Main Street, and from 1928 to 1930, he worked out of 147$^{1/2}$ East Main Street. By 1934 he had moved to 153$^{1/2}$ North Church, the studio for which he is probably best known. His Spartanburg High *Scribbler* advertisement that year announced, "Photographs in This Annual Furnished By Alfred T. Willis." The brick building, which was torn down in the early 1980s, stood between the Hammond-Brown-Jennings furniture store on the corner of St. John and North Church Streets and the present site of Control Data's Business Technology Center at 145 North Church. Alfred Willis continued to work out of that studio until his death.

"Both Alfred and Bob were intent," said Willis family friend Henry DuPre. A teenager at the time, Henry remembers Alfred taking school portraits and photographs of sports teams. In fact, he is pictured in one of Alfred's images of the Spartanburg High basketball team. "He wanted a picture of us in the huddle," Henry remembers, "taken from inside looking up." To get the shot, Alfred asked the boys to balance in formation on top of the parallel bars while he scrambled beneath them and took the photograph. The photo went as planned. As they were climbing down, though, a stray ball hit Alfred's camera

One of the most exciting nights I ever spent was in a sailing boat over near the West Indies, when I'd been in the service just about two months. I had the midnight watch—from twelve 'til two—and I'd just turned in when the wind began to rise, and they shouted, "All hands on deck to shorten sail!" And when they said all hands, they meant everybody, so I crawled out. My yard was at an extreme end of the boat, hanging out over the water, and I scurried up into the rigging and had just shortened the sail when the squall broke. I'd never seen water as high in all my life. One minute I was dipping down so low I could stick out one foot and kick the water, and then in no time I was up where I could have reached out and grabbed a hat full of stars. I wrapped myself around that yard and hung on for about a half hour, and I bet if you were to look at that boat now, you'd still find the impression of my hands in the wood.

—Alfred T. Willis as quoted in the
Spartanburg High School *Scribbler*,
Thursday, May 28, 1936

After Alfred Willis died, his son Bob Willis assumed the role of official Spartanburg County schools' photographer. Bob took this grade-school portrait of his half sister Lib.

and shattered the lens. "Mr. Dobson, who was our coach, wouldn't let anybody say 'damn,'" Henry says, referring to the prohibition against profanity in the gym. The coach immediately began soothing Alfred and offered to buy a replacement. "And Mr. Willis said, 'Well that ain't got a damn thing to do with it. There ain't another one between here and Atlanta. You *can't* buy another one.' And then he just raised hell," Henry recalls, laughing.

Alfred married Lib Willis Fowler's mother, Lucille Miller Willis, after his first wife, Bob's mother, Lelia Blackwell Willis, died in 1928. Eighteen years older than Lucille, Alfred was a longtime friend of her family and even told his four daughters of bouncing their mother as a baby on his knee. A member of the first graduating class from Spartanburg's School of Nursing, Lucille was 40 when their youngest child, Lib, was born; Alfred was 58. His images of a laughing brood of pig-tailed daughters, some of his last, tell the story of an older, much softened father. Often pictured together, the pajama-clad girls hold unwrapped presents up for his camera in their 660 Glendalyn Avenue home on Christmas morning, or giggle beneath crowns of braids while swimming together in Dutchman's Creek.

Struck by a taxi while crossing Main Street at the corner of Oakland Avenue on a Sunday, Alfred Willis lived until the following Tuesday. Lib was in just the first grade and remembers the call her mother received that fateful night in 1945. Her half brother Bob arrived to pick her up from school. "They came and said 'your Daddy's here,'" she remembers. "And being a child, I thought, 'oh boy, Daddy's okay.' But then, of course, it was Bob." Without a male figure in those formative years after Alfred's death, Lib often felt anxious around men. More than twenty years older than Lib and father to a daughter Lib's age, Bob was more of an uncle than brother. Looking back through family photographs, Lib can clearly remember which of her school portraits Bob took, and which are her father's. "I think Bob had the personality my Dad had," she says, "because he loved to laugh and tell tales. He would crack you up." Lib and Bob grew closer as adults. In a grade school portrait of Lib with freshly trimmed bangs and signature plaited pigtails, a dimple nestles in her right cheek. Her wide, open-mouthed smile reveals spaces between new teeth. The photograph, in which she can't help laughing, is Bob's.

An earlier portrait, taken when Lib was one year old, appeared in her father's Willis Studio advertisement in the Spartanburg City Directory. "There were pictures of me from the time I was born up until he died. And of course, as soon as I was old enough to click a camera, my parents bought us little brownie cameras. I just assumed everybody in the world had tons of pictures," she remembers. It's important to note here that Alfred Willis not only started his business but also established himself as a successful commercial photographer in a fragile economic climate. The destruction of more than fifty percent of the cotton crop by the boll weevil in the early 1920s dealt South Carolina a major blow, and its farm-based economy suffered to a greater degree than other states. By the time of the Great Depression in 1929, an agricultural depression had already ransacked the state for eight years. Spartanburg's 30,000 citizens, many of whom had comprised the state's primary labor manufacturing force, were forced out of textile jobs by subsequently closed cotton mills. Even those mills that remained open had to reduce workers' hours and wages significantly. Against a financial backdrop that made the purchase of photographs nearly cost prohibitive, Alfred Willis continued to work.

Fortunately, neither Alfred Willis nor his son Bob after him limited their subjects to people who could afford their services. To their credit are photographs documenting life in mill villages, devastated families relocated from the Camp Croft area, a Depression-era downtown scene with masses of people rushing to banks to withdraw deposits, Converse students boarding a bus to pick cotton during the depleted labor force of World War II, and shotgun houses in Gas Bottom. The photographs reflect a storied period not only in local but also in national history. And when the Willises turned their cameras on the people of Upcountry South Carolina, something beautiful happened. The photographs reveal a community of joy, humor, and dignity, oftentimes in the face of devastating poverty. For example, because Alfred Willis had the wit and foresight to photograph him, future generations will not only know the tales but also the face, hat, hands, and fiddle of Trottin' Sally. Raised in Converse Heights just blocks from the then largely African-American neighborhood

Because Alfred Willis had the good humor and foresight to photograph him, future generations will not only know the tales but also the face, hat, hands, and fiddle of the 1920s downtown entertainer George Mullins, better known as Trottin' Sally.

behind Spartanburg's present YMCA, Bob Willis's longtime neighbor Henry DuPre remembers, "That's where Trottin' Sally would come out. It was pitiful, really. People now don't understand. They had nothing. And I don't know what he did for a living. I guess people would give him a dime or nickel or something like that." Henry leans forward in his chair and laughs, "But he could make that fiddle talk. We'd say, 'Trottin' Sally, make it say *apple pie*.' And just exactly like somebody saying it, he'd make it say *apple pie*."

* * *

Maybe it takes a character to know one, and "old man Alfred T. and Bob were characters," says Henry DuPre. "You don't see many like them anyone." Henry and Bob moved into houses side by side on Palmetto Street in Spartanburg's Converse Heights neighborhood within a month of each other—Bob in December 1946 and Henry in January 1947. Bob had recently taken over his father Alfred's studio, with yearbook photographs comprising most of his business. Henry remembers Bob often worked through the night, sorting 5x7 and 8x10 portraits on his dining room table. "How he turned out the work he did, I don't know," Henry says. For years Bob drove around with the phrase *we photograph anything anywhere anytime* on the side of his jeep. "I don't know why he said we," though, "because there wasn't anybody but Bob Willis." The pair became fast friends. New fathers within months of each other, it wasn't uncommon to see Henry and Bob out strolling fussy babies up and down Palmetto Street together. The almost fifty-year-long friendship grew from there.

"He loved children," Susan Brown says of her grandfather. The Willis and DuPre families, plus two or three nearby households, boasted twelve young children between them. On a typical afternoon, Bob arrived home from work, rounded up the lot, and initiated a parade—a few wagons in front, then tricycles and scooters—which he, of course, conducted through Converse Heights. Two little boys who lived across the street, as Bob's wife, Sue Clary, loved to tell, routinely rang the doorbell to ask if Mr. Willis could come out and play. Bob sowed grass twice a year and used to say that in all his time, he had never done

Bob and Sue Clary Willis moved into 541 Palmetto Street in Converse Heights in December 1946. Family friend and longtime neighbor Henry DuPre, whose house is visible along the far-right side of this photograph, moved next door in January 1947.

it without a child at his side "helping." His ultimate "herd" included not only his own eight grandchildren and five great grandchildren but also neighborhood kids. Children were fixtures at his studio as well—throwing pennies into the developer and making prints of their hind ends, among their favorite pastimes. The year before Bob Willis died at the age of seventy-eight, he bounced around the block on a pogo stick. It's little wonder a man so childlike himself created such magic around him.

But Bob hardly reserved his charm for children. In order to keep up with Bob, his green thumb neighbor, Henry decided one spring to border his yard in impatiens. Everyday Henry watered his new plants; and everyday after he left for work, Bob sneaked over and added new impatiens to Henry's bed. It was months before Henry realized it was not his regimented watering that kept his yard so beautiful. And why throw out a perfectly good Christmas tree for the garbage collectors to pick up? "He made a big deal," Henry remembers, chuckling. Bob waited for his tree to get "dry as a bone, so he could light it at the bottom and make a great big flame. Oh, we did that every Christmas." Many years later Henry, then a widower, married Bob's widowed daughter Patricia. "Henry was always a part of our lives," as Patricia's daughter Susan says, "and now he is taking care of all of us."

Of Bob's relationship with his father Alfred, Henry senses they were not close. When Alfred's first wife, Lelia Blackwell Willis, died in 1928, their four young children—Alfrieda, Mary, William (known as Shag), and Bob—moved in with his parents, Mr. Robert Henry and Mrs. Jessie Thompson Willis, in Simpsonville. Those near to Bob believe that he felt abandoned much of his life. "I think that somehow we benefited, though," Susan offers, describing Bob's children and grandchildren, "because he held onto each one of us so tightly. He couldn't love any of us enough."

Bob adored his grandfather, who was principal teacher at the school in Williston, South Carolina from 1879 until his retirement around the turn of the century. Many Willis children, including Bob and his siblings, boarded at their grandparents' home in order to benefit from his instruction. Henry remembers that his grandfather was a significant influence on Bob. A photograph of the

Discovered in one of the Willis family trunks, this photograph depicts three generations of Robert Henry Willis—"Father" Willis *(left)*, Lieutenant Colonel Robert "Henry" Willis, Jr. *(right)*, and between them, Bob Willis as a toddler.

three generations of Robert Henry Willis was discovered in a Willis family trunk—sage Father Willis with furrowed forehead and white beard, dashing twenty-something Henry on furlough from the army and sporting a mustache, and between them, little Bob giggling, likely at his father Alfred. Robert "Henry" Willis, Jr., not having seen his family in four years, obtained four months' leave in October 1912, the greater part of which he spent with his parents in Simpsonville. It was during those months that many candid photographs of the rarely photographed Alfred, as well as other Willis family members were taken.

Though Bob and his father may not have remained close, Bob grew up watching Alfred and his uncle Henry with cameras. From them he learned an appreciation for technology and throughout his life he sought the latest equipment. "What I love most about Alfred Willis is that he was an enthusiast through and through, a professional who pushed the medium, loved the gadgetry of it, and the technical aspects of it," Carroll Foster says. Henry DuPre remembers that Bob, too, insisted on the best cameras and lenses. "Of course, he also had the first television, the first Volkswagen, and the first Jeep. He had the first of everything that came to Spartanburg." Lib remembers Bob owned a 16mm projector, and the Willises gathered occasionally to watch home movies. Among them is not only a clip of Lib at age four, but a clip of her in color. Introduced in the late 1930s, Kodak offered Kodachrome in 16 mm format. Although it eventually became the first commercially successful color film, at the time, Kodachrome would have been pricey and difficult to obtain. Not for Alfred Willis. Little known to anyone except Willis family members, his popular photograph of Converse College women boarding a bus to pick cotton in October of 1942 was also captured on color film. Lib says she could hardly believe what she was seeing. In a time when even still images were generally shot in black and white, here was a moving, yellow school bus.

Another trait essential to Bob's success as a photographer was his fearlessness. Like Alfred before him, Bob would go to any length for a photograph. As Duke Power's longest continuous contractor, he climbed water tanks, ascended in crane buckets, and even crawled into a boiler in the heart of a coal-fired plant over the course of his forty-something years with the

Bob Willis inherited his father Alfred's 16mm projector, and the Willis family gathered occasionally to watch home movies. Little known to anyone except Willis family members, Alfred's image of Converse College girls loading a bus to pick cotton in October of 1942 was also captured on color film.

company. "I've had to get on hands and knees, dragging my equipment back through tunnels, through boulders and standing water," then seventy-seven-year-old Bob Willis remarked of his typical 16-hour days in a 1991 interview for Duke's monthly employee newsletter. Duke manager Bob Lynn recalled riding in a plane with him to shoot aerial photographs when Willis shouted, "Grab my belt!" The next thing Lynn knew the photographer was hanging out of the door, shooting straight down. Another time Bob flipped his Ford Bronco to avoid hitting two dogs. He then climbed from the wreckage, found his camera and duly photographed the scene. As if that weren't enough action for one day, he then hitched a ride home, borrowed his wife Sue Clary's Buick, and proceeded to the Duke jobsite. Still another time the helicopter in which he was flying crashed. Again, Bob crawled out, dusted off, and photographed the wreckage. In the Duke feature, Bob credited his father, Alfred, with his training. "He never showed me," he said, "I just watched him." Indeed, Bob absorbed much more than just how to mix chemicals and process film. One of his first portraits, a photograph of his childhood Boston terrier Pixie Willis, was taken while he was a young boy living with his grandparents in Simpsonville. As Bob told the *Duke Power News*, "I learned a lot from my daddy."

"I think he took more pictures of the dogs than he did of the children," Lib Fowler surmised of her father Alfred. Indeed, a love for animals, especially dogs, runs in the Willis family. Alfred Willis rarely drove his Chrysler Airflow anywhere without a Boston terrier hanging out of the window. A canine passenger always accompanied Bob, too, in his International Harvester Scout, on which he logged some 312,000 miles. Many Spartanburg locals fondly remember his last two dogs, cocker spaniels Charlie and Zack. Mark Olencki knew to expect Bob when he heard Zack bounding down the Schuyler Building hallway ahead of him. Known as "Photo-Willis" to Duke Power colleagues, Bob traveled at least once a week to construction sites. He sent progress photographs back to Duke, so upper management could keep track of developments onsite without leaving their offices. Beginning in 1949, anywhere Duke Power Company embarked on a major project, Bob Willis and a four-legged companion were there to document it. If you look closely at the estimated 200,000 Willis

Known as "Photo" Willis to Duke Power employees, Bob Willis climbed water tanks, ascended in crane buckets and helicopters, and crawled into a boiler in the heart of a coal-fired plant over the course of his forty-something years with the company. Pictured on site in 1979, Duke's longest continuous contractor always donned his signature hard hat.

photographs of embankments, tunnels, dikes, and dams, you will often spot Charlie in the corner peering back. For fifteen years, Charlie accompanied Bob, and the pair became a legend on Duke sites. Ironically Bob considered cocker spaniels "sissy" dogs, his granddaughter Susan says. He bought a pair named Candy and Charlie—one for his grandson and one for his daughter. "Somehow or another, though, Granddaddy ended up with both of those dogs." Charlie went on to become his traveling companion.

After Charlie died, one of Bob's granddaughters bought him another spaniel named Zack. Like Charlie before him, Zack became a mainstay onsite and even wore a Duke employee badge on his collar. Like those of all employees, his also measured radiation levels. Duke sites weren't the only places Bob took his dogs, though. Dogs often trailed behind him in the post office, bank, and even restaurants. Before the cocker spaniels, Bob owned a Chihuahua named Maggie and carried her in his coat pocket. "You know, people just got to the point where they expected this idiosyncrasy," Susan says, "and his dogs were allowed places where dogs never were."

Even squirrels, which Bob Willis notoriously despised, found themselves humanely relocated from Converse Heights. After capturing them in "have a heart" traps, Bob routinely exported the squirrels to Pauline and other stretches of land on his way to Duke sites. He bragged once that he'd relocated over one hundred squirrels. Like his father before him, Bob loved the outdoors and was a member of the Spartanburg Gun Club. He often took his three daughters—Patricia, Sandra Sue, and Jane Lelia—and grandchildren to the preserve, where he pointed out, among other things, squirrels' nests. Unlike Alfred, though, Bob was never much of a marksman. In fact, his family always suspected he joined the gun club not to hunt but to have a place to walk in the woods.

Among Bob's other quirks was his fondness for homing pigeons, which he kept caged behind his house on Palmetto Street. Each morning he'd take a few to his Church Street studio as a means of communicating with his family. Telephones would have been utterly unimaginative. Susan remembers her grandfather sending a pigeon home to ask of his wife and grandchildren what they would like from the Kennedy Street Hardee's. Another pigeon carried

Bob Willis's granddaughter Susan Brown shared this telegram from Bob to his wife Sue Clary. Sue passed away in May 1992, and Bob in January 1993. Over those eight months he visited her grave every day with a flower.

their lunch orders back to the studio. "I don't know what else to say," Susan says longingly of her grandfather, "he was just magic."

More so than anywhere else, perhaps, Bob's telegrams to his wife Sue Clary illuminate what can only be described as his characteristic zest for life and unabashed affection. "Hey 'Suz'anne Darling," he writes in a delicately folded telegram, now in his granddaughter Susan's possession, "Boy O boy I have certainly been busy. I am up to my eyes in pictures and can hardly write for them. You should be here to dig me out." Always, he signed them quintessentially Bob—"Toodle de ooooooooooooooh," or "Yours till the bench breaks." The woman Henry DuPre describes as "very, very ladylike" never wore a pair of pants and sobbed when Bob taught their young grandchildren to sing, *Oh, it ain't gonna rain no more no more. It ain't gonna rain no more. How in the hell can the old folks tell when it ain't gonna rain no more.* At Bob's funeral, Dr. Alastair Walker claimed that although Bob always had a joke ready for him when they met at the Skillet, he couldn't repeat any of them from the pulpit. Somehow, though, the perpetually even-tempered lady who didn't use the word "legs" unless referring to a chicken and the man who insisted she unplug the refrigerator twenty minutes before his arrival home for lunch, as hearing it run might upset his digestion, had quite the romance. When his wife Sue became ill, Bob commuted to and from Duke Power sites as far away as Virginia in a single day to get back home to her. Mark Olencki wasn't surprised when Bob's heart attack so closely followed Sue Clary's death. She passed away in May 1992, and Bob in January 1993. Over those eight months he visited her grave everyday with a flower. "You know," Mark said, "you hear about couples like that."

SPARTANBURG THROUGH THE LENS

Since stepping foot on Wofford College's campus as a freshman in 1971, Mark Olencki has been watching Spartanburg through his camera lens. Mark recalls a thriving downtown, shopping at JCPenney and Sears, and going to

For 42 years Duke people have known you can't predict when or where "Photo" Willis is going to show up. You may encounter him slogging through mud and boulders 600 feet underground. He may be found on a catwalk inside a power plant. Or on a water tower. Or in a crane. Or leaning fearlessly out of a helicopter door.

Wherever he shows up, he is assured a warm and affectionate greeting from Duke employees. Generations of us have come to admire his work and to regard him with affection and esteem. Willis, his dogs and his photographs are a lasting part of the history and lore of Duke Power. As the only single person to witness and document the modern era of Duke construction, he has earned a place as a legend in our company's history.

—from "'Photo' Willis takes his place along the legends," *Duke Power News*, September 1991, by Jeremy Drier

The Chapman Building, later known as the Andrews Building, was Spartanburg's first skyscraper when it opened in 1912. Primed for demolition in 1977, it accidentally collapsed and killed five workers. Extended Stay America is now located on the site.

see the *The Poseidon Adventure* in the Montgomery Building's Carolina Theater. But even then things downtown were shifting. The last film he can remember seeing there was The Who's 1975 rock opera *Tommy*. When Westgate Mall opened, JCPenney relocated to the West side. Then Hillcrest Mall shot up on the east side, and as Mark says, "Spartanburg became a donut." Before long, Spartanburg's first skyscraper, the Chapman Building (later known as the Andrews Building) was slated for demolition but collapsed on its own in 1977, killing five men.

The 1970s and '80s marked what Mark laments as the gutting of downtown. Imploded to make way for the Spartan Foods tower (now Denny's corporate), the Franklin Hotel was another prominent Spartanburg landmark. Its omission from Main Street, like that of the Chapman Building and others, epitomizes the challenge Carroll and Mark faced in recreating the Willis originals. Although many American cities initiated historic preservation efforts in the 1970s and '80s, Spartanburg didn't get on board until the 1990s. In many cases, it was simply too late. The Twichell house (1882), which stood on the corner of Pine and Glendalyn Streets until its demolition in the 1970s, represents another architectural loss.

Although both Mark and Carroll felt a responsibility to document change, that impulse was matched by an equally strong need to preserve, to prove where the landscape remained whole. On one of his first assignments downtown, Mark glanced at the Willis original in his hand, then up at a building, back at the photograph, and again at the building. Something was off. The windows just weren't lining up. Frustrated, he turned the corner and, "boom, there was the picture. Everything exactly the same, exactly as it was." Mostly, the photographers want to stand in the Willises' shoes. They want to see as Alfred or Bob did when they looked through the lens. As Carroll explained, his best bet in many of the recreated photographs, was to capture the original's vantage point. "You try to stand in the same spot, even if the photographer was on top of a building or hanging out of a window."

Given the adventurous tactics of Alfred and Bob Willis, I shouldn't have been surprised to discover Carroll ascending a service ladder, his camera and upper body disappearing through a hatch in the ceiling on the first day we ventured out together. That afternoon, he needed access to the rooftop of a building that was once the site of the Palmetto Theatre—now home to Café Ishi—so he could shoot the courtyard across the street. It meant that I was going up too. As I gazed across downtown rooftops and church steeples, and upon the campuses of Wofford and Converse Colleges, I thought of the similarities between the Spartanburg Alfred and Bob Willis photographed and this one. After three major renovations, the exterior of Wofford's Old Main building remains faithful to its 1854 design. The same might be said of Twichell Auditorium at Converse. And yet, Spartanburg's topography is embroidered with history—its downtown streets, buildings, and storefronts toppled, reconfigured, and rebuilt as often as a child's set of blocks. I grasped, maybe for the first time, the magnitude of the Willis family legacy, the record they bequeathed. Which might also explain, though a relative newcomer, why so much felt absent to me—the once bustling Franklin Hotel across the street, simply vanished. From the rooftop, I peered into the eerie scorched remnants of a hollowed out building down the street. Then, as now, I thought of how much we have to learn about our sacrifices to progress.

"A lot of Alfred's pictures show Spartanburg with just so many people shopping and hanging out," Carroll says, "and when something big happened like Charles Lindbergh coming to town, I mean everybody was there." After seeing Alfred Willis's photograph of East Main Street bustling with thousands of spectators, I had to agree. On our Thursday outing, downtown felt somehow deserted. Carroll mused, "Oh, those were the glory days of Spartanburg," but quickly added, "but there are glory days now. I love Spartanburg, and I like living here. I want to carry that torch. I want to be a part of the next generation of commercial photography here."

On the way home from one of our excursions, Carroll told me about a dream

On October 12, 1927 a parade and civic dinner were held in honor of Charles Lindbergh's visit to Spartanburg. Thousands of citizens, including Alfred Willis, congregated along East Main Street to catch a glimpse of the national hero.

Just before Alfred and Bob Willis's 153½ North Church Street studio underwent the wrecking ball in the early 1980s, Mark Olencki climbed up and salvaged the Willis Studio commercial sign. It hangs inside Olencki Graphics, Inc. on South Pine Street to this day.

he had in which he stumbled upon a house with a long sloping driveway. An unattended hand truck had begun rolling down. "Well, I went and grabbed it," he said, "and as I started to roll it back up, I realized that the boxes were full of negatives. I started looking through them, and this old black man came out and said, 'Here, son, you can have a few of these. I appreciate you saving them.'" When he told Lib Fowler the dream, her eyes welled with tears—then his did. The man, they agreed, was Trottin' Sally. "It could be just a dream," Carroll admitted, "but this was so important to me. I spent weekends and nights when I had spare time just making sure that when the library got the collection it would be complete." Carroll's respect for the Willis family, and for Lib and Jerry Fowler, is immense. Of his labor of love, Lib Fowler gushes, "he has the patience of Job."

Mark Olencki, too, feels a personal connection with the Willis family. The basement studios he and Bob Willis shared in the Schuyler Building on South Church Street had once served as a darkroom for the Department of Agriculture and had no windows, heat or air. "We never knew if it was day or night," Mark said. Neither Mark nor Bob had much in the way of signage, nor did they anticipate walk-in customers. The multi-use building was a kind of catchall for small businesses. But the rent was cheap. Unmarried then, Mark worked all hours of the day and night, sometimes twenty-four at a time. Bob was working exclusively for Duke Power, and he would tell Mark about setting up 600 feet underground and shooting with his old Hasselblad camera, considered bulky even then. Bob had to send it off every few months for cleaning because of dust on Duke sites. Mark recalls asking Bob how he managed to get such beautiful, crisp photos so far down. Bob probably answered him the same way he did a Duke reporter in 1991. "I just open the shutter, use a flash if I need it, and then shut it." When asked how long he kept the shutter open, Bob didn't know. "I just sort of subconsciously know. I don't have time to think about it. I just do it." Such nonchalance characterized Bob Willis. "He had incredible intuition but was also just an extremely experienced photographer," Mark remembers. "He carried all this knowledge in his head."

On more than one occasion Bob invited Mark to talk with him in his darkroom, where he continued to process film in the pitch black or dodge and burn prints, without missing a beat. Mark never heard Bob utter a cross word. As Mark said, Bob epitomized "the old southern gentlemen." For Mark, who was just beginning his career in commercial photography, Bob Willis served as the ideal role model. And the white-haired photographer and great grandfather, who stood no taller than 5' 2' and used an enlarger twice his size, welcomed the protégé under his wing. Just before the $153^{1/2}$ North Church Street studio underwent the wrecking ball in the early 1980s, Mark climbed up and salvaged the old Willis Studio commercial sign, which hangs inside his Pine Street studio to this day. Anytime he stumbles on portraits bearing the Willis Studio stamp, he buys them for his collection.

* * *

Our hope is that this book, with its newly released Willis family photographs, and, now, the photographs of Carroll Foster and Mark Olencki, will likewise become cherished in Spartanburg's collective history. As new generations encounter the collection, we hope this book lends context, encourages pride in Spartanburg's traditions, and serves as caution against repeating past mistakes. In publishing *Spartanburg Revisited: A Second Look at the Photographs of Alfred and Bob Willis*, we want not only to recognize the legacy of the Willis photographs—to bring them out of storage and down from the library's lobby walls into living rooms and hands—but also to shed light on the colorful and charismatic photographers behind those images.

While this book's immediate relevance and enjoyment are obvious objectives, we also hope, like Alfred and Bob Willis's photographs, that this new set of images becomes richer with time. "It's not just a book for today," as Carroll has said, "but a book to be appreciated through the years." When people, a century from now, want to know what it felt like to live and work in Spartanburg, may they turn to the photographs of Alfred and Bob Willis, Mark Olencki and Carroll Foster.

Spartanburg supporters built a temporary "temple" for a six-week religious revival led by evangelist Billy Sunday in 1922. The structure was subsequently dismantled and its wood sold, but not before 7,000 people passed through its doors and Alfred Willis was there to document the event.

The trolley era was coming to a close in 1935, and only one car, which ran to Clifton, was still in operation. City buses are lined up in Morgan Square, waiting for passengers. —*Alfred Willis*

Now cars pass through the redesigned greenspaces and fountains of Morgan Square where horses, then trolleys, then buses once came. —*Mark Olencki*

Alfred Willis once owned this home near the corner of Dean and Union streets. When the property was sold in 1917 for the Jewish synagogue, Alfred and a hired team of horses relocated the house farther down the street. —*Alfred Willis*

The Jewish community and its three dozen members constructed the Temple B'nai Israel in 1917. The new Temple on Heywood Avenue opened in 1963, and most recently, this building was used by the Bread of Life Christian Fellowship. —*Carroll Foster*

The American Legion World Series was held in front of a packed stadium at Duncan Park in 1936. The Spartanburg team *(left)* defeated the team from Los Angeles that year. None of the Spartanburg players was more than 17 years old. —*Alfred Willis*

Members of the Spartanburg Stingers baseball team gathered for a group photograph on July 6, 2006, in what could be the last year of play at Duncan Park. The park was padlocked after this game because of maintenance issues. —*Carroll Foster*

First National Bank constructed this office on the corner of Main and Magnolia and operated it until the Great Depression. C&S Bank reopened it in 1933, and when it finally closed in 1991, it was the longest continually operating bank in Spartanburg. —*Alfred Willis*

Justin's Steakhouse, which opened in the spring of 2007, is the latest restaurant tenant in the old bank building. —*Mark Olencki*

The Hotel Franklin, which opened in 1923, had an elegant first-floor dining room and ballroom. In the 1970s the hotel, which was on the National Register of Historic Places, fell on hard times and became a boarding house. It also housed the popular Hooley's nightclub, owned by Bobby Cudd. —*The Willis Collection*

The old hotel was imploded in September 1991 to make room for the tallest building ever constructed in downtown Spartanburg. Denny's Corporation now operates its worldwide chain of restaurants from this $25 million structure. —*Carroll Foster*

West Main was a tree-lined street when Alfred Willis took this photograph in 1925. The Cleveland Hotel, which stood at the western end of Morgan Square, is pictured at top left. The iron fence kept people from falling into the ravine on the south side of the street. —*Alfred Willis*

Today this part of town is home to several automotive businesses. City leaders hope that the ravine, behind the Auto Fleet, can one day become a park or a lake. —*Mark Olencki*

Two unidentified young men in a roadster —*Alfred Willis*

Mayor Bill Barnet, at the wheel, and City Councilman Ken Smith drive a BMW Z3 roadster to the site of the former Spartan Mills. The Z3 car is one of 300,000 manufactured at the vehicle assembly plant in Spartanburg County between 1996 and 2002. —*Carroll Foster*

Converse College and the surrounding neighborhoods from the air, sometime around 1943. —*Alfred Willis*

The campus, which serves more than 1,700 graduate and undergraduate students,
has filled in with buildings and mature hardwood trees. —*Carroll Foster*

The First Baptist Church constructed this Romanesque Revival church campus in 1904.
It was destroyed in a dramatic fire on November 13, 1962. —*Alfred Willis*

A replacement church rose from the ashes and opened exactly four years later, on November 13, 1966.
First Baptist moved into the television age that day, broadcasting the first church service in color in South Carolina. —*Carroll Foster*

James Bivings built his home in Glendale, then known as Bivingsville, in 1830. By the mid-1850s, the mill's second owner, John Bomar, lived there. —*Alfred Willis*

Empty since the 1970s, the Bomar house awaits restoration. —*Mark Olencki*

Bob Willis photographed the intersection of South Converse and Henry Streets sometime around 1960.
Southern Railway no longer ran through here, though the ruts in the street remain.
The city water tank, built in 1935, is visible above the neighborhood. —*Bob Willis*

This once-walkable neighborhood was gradually replaced by wide streets, a gas station, and a 700-car parking deck. —*Carroll Foster*

The Gas Bottom neighborhood, located near the intersection of what is now South Pine Street and Daniel Morgan Avenue, was home to 300 families—most of them African American—as well as an odorous gas plant. Much of this neighborhood was demolished in urban renewal in the early 1960s. —*The Willis Collection*

A community baseball diamond took the place of the neighborhood but was sold by the city in the early 1980s to Vic Bailey for his burgeoning car and truck sales business. This section of Daniel Morgan Avenue is now known as Vic Bailey Boulevard in honor of his service to the S.C. Department of Transportation. —*Carroll Foster*

Spartanburg's art-deco-style Greyhound Bus terminal stood on the corner of North Liberty and Dunbar streets. It opened in 1940. —*Alfred Willis*

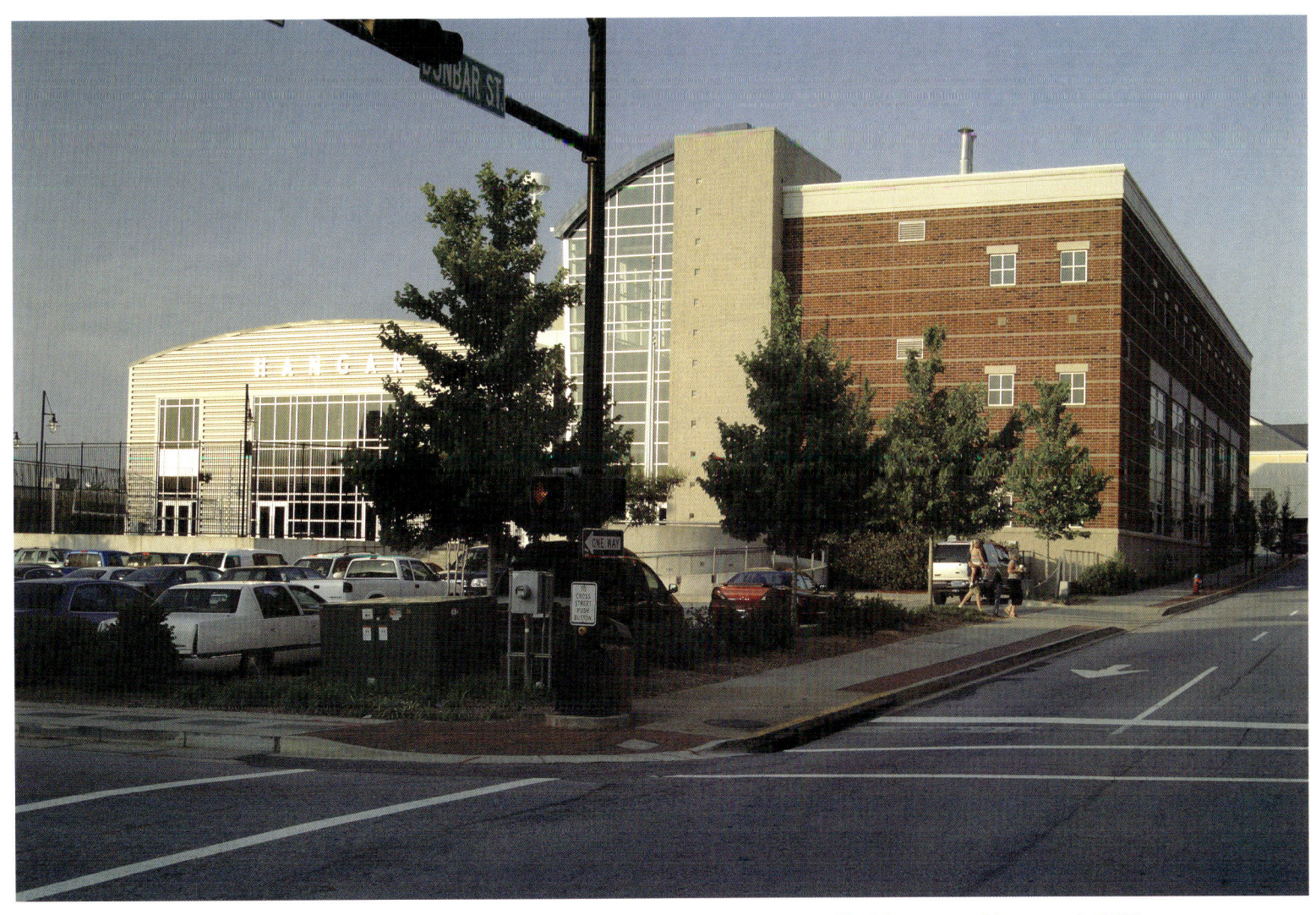

The First Baptist Church opened its $7.9 million student center, known as The Hangar, on this corner in 2003. Among its many amenities, the building has a 950-seat flexible auditorium, a radio broadcast booth, a 3-on-3 basketball court and an authentic T-28 Navy fighter plane hanging from the ceiling. —*Mark Olencki*

The Hammond-Brown-Jennings furniture store was founded in 1907 by George C. Brown and W. Furman Wall, who were later joined by Charlie Hammond and Thomas A. Jennings. These 1930s-era vehicles are parked at the store's loading dock on the back side of the business. —*The Willis Collection*

The downtown furniture store is vacant these days, but Hammond-Brown-Jennings has entered its second century of business from a store located in the city's Pinewood area. —*Carroll Foster*

Alfred Willis often took portraits of ordinary citizens he met on the streets of Spartanburg. —*Alfred Willis*

Willie Mayes poses for a photograph with his bike on Broad Street, May 2007. —*Carroll Foster*

Ligon's Drug Store was headquartered at Church at Main in this photograph from the early 1940s. —*Alfred Willis*

An entire block of buildings was removed to make way for "progress" in the 1970s. For 30 years this area, known as Opportunity Block, remained vacant. Finally, in 2005, Extended Stay America built its corporate headquarters on the west side of North Church Street. A fountain now takes the place of Ligon's Drug Store. —*Carroll Foster*

Six years after the conclusion of the Civil War, Spartanburg's first bank—The First National Bank of Spartanburg—opened its doors. Then in 1915 it built this "handsome structure" on Morgan Square. This photograph dates from the 1920s. —*Alfred Willis*

Carolina Gallery, operated by Ed and Shannon Emory, now occupies this building. Art is housed on all three floors. —*Mark Olencki*

This photo is among those in the Willis Collection, but it is debatable whether it was taken by Alfred Willis. Dated in the early 1900s, perhaps it was just one of Alfred Willis's favorite images. Storefronts included Greenewald's, Globe Sample Co., Spiegel Jewelers, Montgomery Crawford and C.D. Kenney Co. —*The Willis Collection*

This stretch of buildings remains the centerpiece of historic downtown Spartanburg. While the square has undergone numerous makeovers, many of these structures remain standing after more than a century of use. —*Carroll Foster*

The cornerstone for the church of St. Paul The Apostle was laid October 14, 1883 on North Dean Street in order to provide a place to worship for a growing Catholic community in Spartanburg. The sanctuary was built as miniature replica of St. Patrick's Catholic Church in Charleston and features buttresses three feet thick. —*Alfred Willis*

The exterior of the old church was sandblasted and repainted in 1974. Plans are in motion to replace this small sanctuary with a much larger one closer to Main Street. —*Mark Olencki*

The Chero-Cola truck was a common sight on Morgan Square in the 1920s. Bottled for many years on Liberty Street, Chero was owned by James B. Fitzgerald and was a competitor to emerging regional powerhouse Coca-Cola. —*Alfred Willis*

Coca-Cola proved to have staying power. J.W. Allen opened the Spartanburg bottling plant in 1903 behind his confectionary store on the western end of Morgan Square. Coca-Cola still serves Spartanburg from a bottling plant on West Main Street. —*Carroll Foster*

The Aug. W Smith Co., a fine department store that was founded in Abbeville in 1890, opened its Spartanburg store in 1900 and moved to this large building in 1925. Its downtown reign came to an end in 1981, followed by the closings of its stores at Westgate and Hillcrest within three years. —*The Willis Collection*

Although Aug. Smith and the Palmetto Theatre (1941-1970) are gone, farther down the street, Smith's Drugs and Kosch & Gray Jewelers still operate. Bishop's Furniture has operated in the former department store building since 1984. —*Carroll Foster*

Built with slave labor, Wofford College's "Old Main" opened in 1854, providing classrooms for the young men who attended the Methodist college. This photograph was taken about 1940. —*Alfred Willis*

Remodeled in 2006 at a cost of $6 million, Wofford's Main Building remains the central feature of the campus, which now serves 1,400 undergraduate students from all over the United States. —*Mark Olencki*

The original Green Street Baptist Church was built to serve the "operatives" at Spartan Mills in 1891. A larger church was built in 1901 and burned in 1928. This structure on Brawley Street replaced that church. —*The Willis Collection*

Today, Green Street Baptist Church, led by the Rev. Tom Moore, serves about 225 members who come from all over the county. —*Carroll Foster*

This photograph was among those in the second Willis Collection recently turned over to the Spartanburg County Public Libraries. The man and the location are unidentified. It is questionable whether he could have landed a fish caught on this flimsy stick! —*Alfred Willis*

Jesse Martin, a resident of Duncan Park, fishes in his neighborhood lake. —*Carroll Foster*

Before the Federal Building was constructed on Magnolia Street in 1931, a string of billboards lined the block. The Montgomery Building and the steeple of Central Methodist Church are visible at the end of what was then called Walnut Street and is now known as Donald S. Russell Street. —*Alfred Willis*

The U.S. Post Office was located here for more than 30 years. The building now houses the
U.S. District Court and a variety of federal offices. —*Mark Olencki*

Alfred Willis stood atop the Cleveland Hotel in the 1930s to photograph Morgan Square, which featured a bandstand at the upper end and a traffic island at the lower end to handle the increasing number of cars. —*Alfred Willis*

Morgan Square was overhauled again in 2006, with widened sidewalks and the relocation of the statue of Daniel Morgan to its original site. The clock tower, which has stood since the sesquicentennial year of 1981, received new landscaping.   *Carroll Foster*

The staff of the U.S. Post Office in Spartanburg posed for Alfred Willis in front of their mail truck sometime in the 1920s. —*Alfred Willis*

Spartanburg mail carriers, 2007 —*Carroll Foster*

Road construction was underway in the early 1920s on what became known as St. John Street. The two-story brick building just beyond the railroad overpass was the Hastoc School, founded in 1907 to educate an exclusive clientele of Spartanburg boys, some of whom boarded on the second floor. —*Alfred Willis*

St. John Street is now the gateway to the Chapman Cultural Center, whose grand opening took place in October 2007. City leaders hope the land surrounding the arts complex will one day be home to offices, retail stores, and downtown housing. —*Carroll Foster*

Four trains are loading passengers at the Union Station on Magnolia Street in this 1930s photograph: the Carolina Special, northbound and southbound; and the Piedmont Limited, headed east and west. —*Alfred Willis*

The Southern Crescent is the only passenger train that stops in Spartanburg anymore, stopping northbound and southbound after dark. Plenty of freight trains, like this one, continue to barrel through. —*Carroll Foster*

Downtown Spartanburg, from the south, circa 1943 —*Alfred Willis*

Downtown Spartanburg, 2007 —*Carroll Foster*

The federal government built this USO club on North Church Street in the early 1940s to provide recreation services to uniformed military personnel, particularly the 300,000 soldiers who trained at Camp Croft. This was one of five USO clubs in Spartanburg County, and the only one built from scratch. —*The Willis Collection*

The law offices of Burts, Turner, Rhodes and Thompson are now located on this corner.
The old Spartan Hotel, soon to undergo renovation, is still visible behind it. —*Mark Olencki*

These two unidentified young women were playing sandlot softball on the grounds of the old Spartanburg High School on Kennedy Street, now known as the Evans Resource Center. —*Alfred Willis*

Jaynay Jones *(left)* and Tierra Smith warm up before a Spartanburg High School junior varsity softball game. —*Carroll Foster*

In the 1940s the corner of Main and Church was anchored by Stein's Department store. Other businesses in the area included Ligon's Drugs, William Ornduff, Kinney Shoes, Belk Hudson, Woolworth, Kosch & Gray Jewelers and two movie theaters: The Strand and The Palmetto. Ligon's moved here in the late 1940s and was in business until the mid-1970s. —*Bob Willis*

Ground-floor retail stores on Main Street have been replaced by offices, including the headquarters of McMillan Smith Architects, Upstate Forever, and the City of Spartanburg Economic Development Department. Upper floors of the Palmetto Building have been renovated by Longleaf Development into high-end apartments. —*Mark Olencki*

An unidentified man washes his black Model T Ford. —*Alfred Willis*

Donnie Harrison, a downtown resident, washes his black 2002 Ford Thunderbird convertible along Wall Street. —*Mark Olencki*

Walter S. Montgomery, son of the founder of Spartan Mills, built this elegant home on South Pine Street in the early 1900s, and Montgomery family members lived there until the late 1930s. Cudd & Coan Insurance converted it to business use in 1950. —*Bob Willis*

Mid-South Management has owned this building for more than 20 years. Its real estate operations, as well as those of Orion Properties, are headquartered there. —*Carroll Foster*

Dean Street School opened in 1891 to serve the city's black children. When this photo was taken, the school was known as Alexander Elementary and continued to serve black children. —*The Willis Collection*

The old school house is now occupied by the Omega Fraternity and is used for neighborhood community functions. —Mark Olencki

The ten-story Montgomery Building was constructed at Church and St. John in 1923 and was the original Spartanburg home of Lockwood-Greene Architects. The Carolina Theatre hosted Hollywood movies and live theatre for more than 50 years here. —*Alfred Willis*

Mostly empty for decades, the Montgomery Building awaits a new developer who can restore it to its former glory. Across the street, the J M Smith Corporation has built a downtown park.
—*Carroll Foster*

Bethel Methodist Church was organized in 1856. This church was built in 1907 at the corner of South Church and Lee Streets. It was demolished in 1967. —*The Willis Collection*

When the old church was demolished, it made room for a parking lot to serve the many church members who now drove to church, rather than walked. The new sanctuary, which faces East Henry Street, was built in 1953. —*Mark Olencki*

John F. Floyd established Floyd's Mortuary in Spartanburg in 1886. In the 1920s he decided to convert his home on North Church into a mortuary. —*The Willis Collection*

The J.F. Floyd Mortuary is the oldest and largest business of its kind in the county, handling more than 800 funerals a year, according to its general manager, Russel Floyd. —*Mark Olencki*

Alfred Willis would have been standing on the Southern Railway train trestle to get this photograph of Converse Mill sometime about 1930. Converse Mill, once one of the largest cotton mills in the country, operated for about 80 years until it closed around 1972. —*Alfred Willis*

Tall trees partially obscure the automobile bridge (Highway 29 leading to Cowpens) over the Pacolet River and much of the Converse Mill itself. An out-of-state developer has purchased the old mill and hopes to convert it to residential units. —*Carroll Foster*

Alfred Willis had a fascination with motorcycles. —*Alfred Willis*

Ashley Fly, the patron saint of Spartanburg, and his BMW cycle on the bridge at Glendale. —*Carroll Foster*

Ernest Burwell ran a Chevrolet dealership on the corner of West Main and Daniel Morgan in the early 1940s when this photograph was taken. —*The Willis Collection*

The Chevrolet business moved to North Church Street in the 1960s, and the building burned to the ground in the mid-1980s. A parking lot serving Carriage House Wines and the emerging "Little Ezell Street" restaurant district has replaced it. —*Mark Olencki*

Dr. James Bivings, founder of the textile mill in Glendale, built his home on North Church Street in 1854. He later sold this Greek Revival home to John H. Evins, who was a member of the S.C. Legislature during the Civil War. —*The Willis Collection*

The home was placed on the National Register of Historic Places in 1970. Its current occupants are attorney Alex Evins (great-grandson of its former owner), his wife, Jennifer, and their two children. The servants' quarters and kitchen building remain intact behind the house. —*Mark Olencki*

Mechanics from Pierce Motor Company, the Spartanburg Ford dealership, posed for a photograph in the 1950s. This business, along with an Esso station, was operated by Thomas B. Pierce at the corner of Church and Broad (where the headquarters of the Spartanburg County Public Libraries now stands). The Pierce family sold the franchise in the late 1960s. —*Bob Willis*

Wakefield Buick Pontiac GMC, established in 1945, is now the longest-running car dealership in the city. Mechanics in this photograph, left to right, are: Blake Phillips, Will Reynolds, Nick Slonim *(front)*, Barry Neal, Jerry Stone *(top)*, Mike McGaha, Will Bailey, Richard Bouchard. —*Carroll Foster*

Albert F. Twichell built his mansion on South Pine Street in 1882. Originally from Vermont, Twichell came to Spartanburg to run the cotton mill in Glendale with his brother-in-law, Dexter Edgar Converse. A lover of music, he organized the annual Festival of Music at Converse College. The auditorium is named for him. —*Alfred Willis*

The Fretwell family lived in the old mansion in the mid 20th century. When they moved out, the house was demolished in the late 1970s. Regions Bank built its Spartanburg headquarters there. —*Mark Olencki*

The north side of West Main Street at Spring Street, 1940s. —*The Willis Collection*

This set of buildings, currently owned by Johnson Development, now houses The Pink Bee clothing store and McGarity Gilmore Forrester Architects Inc. —*Mark Olencki*

In 1945 City Hall housed the city manager, the finance department, police and jails, a health department, purchasing, a courtroom and a radio dispatcher. This building was constructed on Broad Street in 1907, replacing the 1820s-era County Jail. —*The Willis Collection*

The 1961 City Hall, built in the International Modernist style of architecture, was constructed on the site of the 1907 building. City offices have once again outgrown their headquarters, and the Spartanburg City Council hopes to replace this structure soon. —*Carroll Foster*

Crowds and trolleys gather on October 10, 1927 to welcome aviator Charles Lindberg to town. —*Alfred Willis*

Seventy-five antique and classic cars and trucks filled Morgan Square June 30, 2007,
as the 25th annual coast-to-coast Great American Race made a stop in Spartanburg. —*Mark Olencki*

Nine members of the 1926 police force: *(front from left)* Mitchell Allen, Jack Alverson, Wideman Bryant and John Thomas; *(back from left)* Joe Holt, Edward Huntly, *(an unidentified man)*, Homer Gresham, and Nick Carter. —*Alfred Willis*

The Police Division of the Spartanburg Public Safety Department gathers for a portrait on the steps of Wofford College's Main Building, June 2007. —*Mark Olencki*

The Valley Falls Mill manufactured yarn along the banks of the Lawson's Fork north of Spartanburg for 135 years. Water from the mill pond flowed over a picturesque dam in this photograph from about 1930. —*Alfred Willis*

The mill, like so many others in Spartanburg County, was demolished about 2002. The area is returning to what it looked like before the textile industry came to the Upstate in the 19th century. Even the mill pond is gone. —*Mark Olencki*

Willis Family Album

Although surviving family members are not certain, this photograph is believed to picture the old home place of
Mr. Robert Henry and Mrs. Jessie Thompson Willis in Simpsonville, South Carolina.

F.co DeAngelis
VIA DELLA POSTA NUOVA 31   MESSINA

Before becoming a commercial photographer, Alfred Willis embarked a four-year naval career that included stints in Europe, Arabia, Ethiopia, and also in the Spanish-American War. This 1903 photograph, taken in Messina, Sicily, shows Alfred in his early twenties.

Alfred's parents, Professor Robert Henry and Mrs. Jessie Thompson Willis. Many Willis children, including Bob and his siblings, lived with their grandparents in order to benefit from Father Willis's instruction. Before retiring to Simpsonville, he was principal teacher at the school in Williston, South Carolina, from 1879 until the turn of the century.

Alfred with first wife, Lelia Evelyn Blackwell Willis.

Alfred Willis had four children with his first wife, Lelia. Pictured *(left to right)* are Alfreda Evelyn Willis Tweed, Mary Josephine Willis Moore, Robert Henry "Bob" Willis, and William Copeland "Shag" Willis.

Not having seen his family in four years, Alfred's brother Lieutenant Colonel Robert "Henry" Willis, Jr. obtained four months' leave in 1912, the greater part of which he spent with his parents in Simpsonville. Here he stands on a train platform with children thought to be his nephew, Bob, and niece, Alfreda.

These candid photographs, likely taken during Henry's four-month furlough from the Army, bring Alfred's sense of humor to light. They feature brothers Alfred, Henry, and George Willis. Known for story telling, the Willises loved to laugh and joke.

Alfred pictured with daughter Mary in his lap. Note the horse-drawn wagons in the background.

An early photograph of Mary Willis hugging her younger brother, Bob

Mary and Bob Willis, brother and sister, test their balance on roller skates. Even as an adult, Bob was known to conduct parades of children on tricycles, scooters, and skates through Converse Heights. The year before he died at the age of seventy-eight, he bounced around the block on a pogo stick.

Both Alfred and Bob Willis insisted on the latest in cars, cameras, photography equipment, and all manner of gadgetry. Here, Alfred poses on the hood of a roadster.

Alfred Willis sets up his camera outside of Spartan High School.

Siblings Alfreda, William "Shag" and Bob Willis

Bob Willis, standing, and his brother, "Shag," roll snowballs

Alfreda and Mary Willis in the snow

Bob *(with Boston Terrier Pixie)*, Alfreda, Mary, and William "Shag," dressed up for a family portrait on the beach

William "Shag," Bob, Mary, and Alfreda pose with armloads of schoolbooks.

A Willis family roadside picnic

Alfred poses with his second wife, Lucille Miller Willis.

Alfred Willis had four daughters with his second wife, Lucille. Here, the pajama-clad girls hold unwrapped presents up for his camera in their Converse Heights home on Christmas morning. Pictured *(left to right)* are Elizabeth "Lib" Willis Fowler, Lucille "Lucy" Willis Graham, Rachael Willis Tuck, and Edith Willis Marsh.

One of Bob Willis's first portraits, a photograph of his childhood Boston Terrier "Pixie Willis," was taken while he was a boy living with his grandparents in Simpsonville.

PIXIE. WILLIS.   Pixie. Willi

Swimming together in Dutchman's Creek was one of the Willis girls' favorite pastimes. Giggling beneath crowns of braids are Rachael, Edith, Lucy, and Lib *(left to right)*.

Alfred with one of the family's many Boston terriers.

Photographed in his studio are Alfred's daughters Lucy, Edith, Rachael and Lib.

ACKNOWLEDGEMENTS

This book would not have been possible without the support of Alfred T. and Bob Willis's surviving children and grandchildren, especially Lib Willis Fowler and her husband, Jerry, and Susan Hayes Brown, who enthusiastically opened their homes, trunks, albums, and hearts to us for this project. Also, Alfred T. Willis's grandson John Tennyson Moore added significantly to the family history and contributed many of the Willis family photographs. For their generosity and candor every step of the way, we express our deep gratitude. Bob Willis's longtime next-door neighbor, Henry DuPre, also offered invaluable insight into both father and son. As Susan said when she introduced us to him, "Henry is a goldmine of history." This book would be incomplete without his knowledge, enthusiasm, and gift for storytelling.

BIOGRAPHIES

Carroll Foster is a master photographer in terms of both creative and commercial images. After graduating from the Savannah School of Art & Design (SCAD), he spent three years working with a fine art photographer in New Mexico, then spent several years with a successful commercial photography studio in South Carolina. Perhaps the desert horizon in New Mexico influenced his eye for the vibrant colors found in his photographs—when he looks through his camera lens, the mundane rolls away to reveal rich texture and color...things most of us wouldn't notice, let alone succeed in capturing photographically. As a result of his artistic nature, solid technical abilities, state-of-the-art software and equipment, he provides highly effective studio and location photography. He is the owner of Hot Eye Photography in Spartanburg.

Mark Olencki is an artist, designer, and photographer with more than three decades of experience in Spartanburg. His photography has appeared in *Fourth Genre*, *National Geographic's Heart of a Nation*, numerous regional, national, and international trade publications, magazines, newspapers, and many Hub City books. In 2000, Mark was selected for a Spartanburg artists' exchange program with the city of Winterthur, Switzerland, and exhibited his photographs in both cities. His photographs have been included in the permanent collection of the state of South Carolina, as well as the private collections of many businesses and individuals. Mark is a 1975 Magna Cum Laude graduate of Wofford College and operates a photo/graphic design studio in Spartanburg, Olencki Graphics, Inc., and has been the book designer for Holocene Press, Wofford College, and thirty Hub City titles.

A native of York, South Carolina, **Emily L. Smith** holds a bachelor's degree in English from Davidson College and a Master of Fine Arts in creative writing from the University of North Carolina Wilmington. Her place-based writing has appeared in the journals *Columbia Poetry Review*, *Front Porch*, *The Journal*, *Smartish Pace*, and *Tar River Poetry*, among others. A former Byington Fellow, she currently directs The Publishing Laboratory at UNCW, where she also teaches. In 2006-07 she lived and wrote in Spartanburg as the Hub City Writers Project's inaugural Writer-in-Residence.

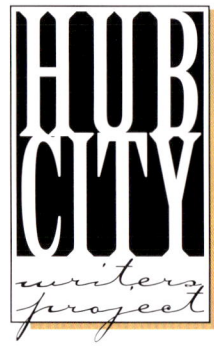

The Hub City Writers Project is a non-profit organization whose mission is to foster a sense of community through the literary arts. We do this by publishing books from and about our community; encouraging, mentoring, and advancing the careers of local writers; and seeking to make Spartanburg a center for the literary arts.

Our metaphor of organization purposely looks backward to the nineteenth century when Spartanburg was known as the "hub city," a place where railroads converged and departed. At the beginning of the twenty-first century, Spartanburg has become a literary hub of South Carolina with an active and nationally celebrated core group of poets, fiction writers, and essayists. We celebrate these writers—and the ones not yet discovered—as one of our community's greatest assets. William R. Ferris, former director of the Center for the Study of Southern Cultures, says of the emerging South, "Our culture is our greatest resource. We can shape an economic base … And it won't be an investment that will disappear."

TITLES

Hub City Anthology • John Lane & Betsy Wakefield Teter, editors

Hub City Music Makers • Peter Cooper

Hub City Christmas • John Lane & Betsy Wakefield Teter, editors

New Southern Harmonies • Rosa Shand, Scott Gould, Deno Trakas, George Singleton

The Best of Radio Free Bubba • Meg Barnhouse, Pat Jobe, Kim Taylor, Gary Phillips

Family Trees: The Peach Culture of the Piedmont • Mike Corbin

Seeing Spartanburg: A History in Images • Philip Racine

The Seasons of Harold Hatcher • Mike Hembree

The Lawson's Fork: Headwaters to Confluence • David Taylor, Gary Henderson

Hub City Anthology 2 • Betsy Wakefield Teter, editor

Inheritance • Janette Turner Hospital, editor

In Morgan's Shadow • A Hub City Murder Mystery

Eureka Mill • Ron Rash

The Place I Live • The Children of Spartanburg County

Textile Town • The Hub City Writers Project

Come to the Cow Pens! • Christine Swager

Noticing Eden • Marjory Heath Wentworth

Noble Trees of the South Carolina Upstate • Mark Dennis, John Lane, Mark Olencki

Literary South Carolina • Edwin Epps

Magical Places • Marion Peter Holt

When the Soldiers Came to Town • Susan Turpin, Carolyn Creal, Ron Crawley, James Crocker

Twenty: South Carolina Poetry Fellows • Kwame Dawes, editor

The Return of Radio Free Bubba • Meg Barnhouse, Pat Jobe, Kim Taylor

Hidden Voices • Kristofer Neely, editor

Wofford: Shining with Untarnished Honor • Doyle Boggs, JoAnn Mitchell Brasington, Phillip Stone, editors

South of Main • Beatrice Hill, Brenda Lee, compilers

Cottonwood Trail • Thomas Webster, G.R. Davis, Jr., Peter L. Schmunk

Courageous Kate • Sheila Ingle

Comfort & Joy • Kirk H. Neely, June Neely Kern

Colophon

A strong sense of déjà vu permeated the creation and production of *Spartanburg Revisited*, the third large-format, full-color Hub City coffeetable "urban nature book." Not only did the photographers, Carroll Foster and Mark Olencki, walk with the Willises visually, but the book design programs and computers are still in the neo-Luddite versions of Mac OS 9.2 and Pagemaker 7.0. Hey, they are good tools and they work! New Nikon D2x cameras utilizing both NEF and JPG formats were the photographers' choice during the year-long photo session. The text face is Bodoni and the display face is Copperplate 29ab with a little Edwardian Script thrown in for fun. The hardback first edition is 300 with an additional softback edition of 3000. Production meetings were held on the balcony of the Wild Wing Cafe (in the historic and renovated Greenewald's building) overlooking Morgan Square and at the Nu-Way Lounge (established in 1938) on Kennedy Street and home of the "Redneck Cheeseburger."